# ODDS & ENDS

*50 Poems That Mean Absolutely NOTHING*

F.L. Riker

authorHOUSE

*AuthorHouse™*
*1663 Liberty Drive*
*Bloomington, IN 47403*
*www.authorhouse.com*
*Phone: 833-262-8899*

*Published by AuthorHouse  01/12/2022*

*ISBN: 978-1-6655-4746-8 (sc)*
*ISBN: 978-1-6655-4745-1 (e)*

# THE GAME

Isolation is the absence of insanity
Insanity is the cure for isolation

It was another day I wasn't there, yet again, no way

They say I was, I thought I was, but no, it was another day

Here I am again, just another day another time and as usual, another day, my watch says Monday

I thought I did this already, oh well, just another day

I keep going around, it's happening again, just another day

Why won't they let me stop, I can't get off the time wheel just another day.

Looking for a place to die
The faster I go the behinder I get
I pause and I try to stand in place
It won't let me die but I can't understand why.

The reasons are plenty and hard on my mind
Looking for the beauty for a weathered mind
My mind is in turmoil, no place to go
I'm stuck in this twilight zone, just can't unwind.

I've travelled the lonesome highways now back to where it all began
A place on the map where no one has been
I'm here and in there can't find my way out
Frozen in time to bare much more than I can.

F.L. RIKER

Crazy is only a place in the mind
In some it's a point of no return
It lies at the center, a place hidden from all
In the whole world just one of a kind.

In me there is no turning back
The crazy is in me to stay
I'll cherish this time for what its worth
All the time would amount to one sharpened tack.

Oh yes, I'm crazy, I've always been there
It makes me do weird things, write dumb thoughts,
And stays with me for one more day.
In the time it takes to write this poem, 20 crazy thoughts just lift me off the bed
I'll wake up this morning to meet this crazy one more time,
And it will take me, again and again I'll go, but this time, to where.

Oh yes, I'm still running, running from the ghost inside me
They hurt sometimes, the pain is hurting in my soul
The faces I killed, the minds I wasted, they're in me I see
I want to go back, back again to pay my toll.

Another state, another state of mind, another place to hide
It never stops, the pain keeps me going, it's in me, I want to go back, back to
where it all began
To face the ghost, to say I'm sorry, but I can't, the pain is just too wide
The ghost gives out the pain, this pain is forever by my side.

This fight will never finish, its taking me down to the bitter end
I can't give up, its just not in me
I may have to kill again, but it hurts so deep within
I have an open passport, a passport to hell for me they send.

There are scars on my brain that will never really heal
The scars of past loves and war
Never healing legacy that are here for eternity
Is me all over again like a rotten orange to peel.

There is nothing left of me, all been taken to the core, stripped to the empty
shell I am
Nothing left to harvest, a barren landscape to sow
The end of a man with no home, here lam no more
All that lam is gone now, more than you could know.

The end is near, I can smell it
The smell of death is part of me
I know what's inside, the intense burning of fear
A familiar odor in my belly, deep in the pit.

I wasn't meant to go, but here I am, and that's that
Another way of life this bitter cold
I need to have my head cleared.
Its getting cold outside, getting frost on my beard, and I forgot my hat.

I've hitch hiked across the country
Lived in every state as I went
Weirdos I ran into are plenty
Problems I had were hell bent.

I have stories I can tell to the avid listener
Stories that would chill you to the bone
Stories that left me one step behind
Trying to catch up to where I belong
I'll tell one more story then try to unwind.

The universe is filled with an empty space, far passed the stars and way beyond
I've been passed the stars on my way home and I'll do it again in a quest to find peace
I've been way out there in an effort to find a way out
Find a way out from the burning memories that possess me and just won't cease

In the empty space they'll have nothing to feed on
The memories will just cease to exist
What a pleasure to dream on this long arrested hope
A time with no memories, a chance to live on.

Dying must be easy, I practice every day
Wipe all useful thoughts from your mind and the rest will fade away
I've died so many times before but never got far enough
One day I'll make it, my thoughts will take me home and there I'll stay

I look up at the stars at night and dream of home so far away
Past the stars and all that matter is a place where I should be
In that distant realm I wonder; I've walked this far you see
The stars will be in place, then I'll do the dying on that day.

You don't have to pray, there's no one out that far
No one to hear but you on your way home to where you'd rather be
Can't talk to people here, they just can't understand
The ways of death are part of me, past the stars where only I can see.

I'll never see the light of day
The sun is only an image to remember
These dark clouds are always in my way
The dark clouds from my past that keep me under.

In my past there are memories that no one should see
In me it's the binding of my soul
The painful memories that I can't forget
I keep on going, but the why is always in me.

It's almost Christmas, must find something to send
My heart is always an option, but a good look shows it's still on the mend
Something new is needed; I'll have to search around
Need new memories I can share, but now that's not too sound

The presents keep on coming, don't even know from where
I have to change the channel, find something new that I can share
The channel I'm on is getting old, the presents have all been returned
Need new memories I can hold, and all new presents to bare.

A picket fence may be what I need but no, that's going too far
A marriage is out of the question, I've been there many times before
One more time may kill me and I do get rather sore
Must keep the rhythm going, and so there will be more.

I sit on this fence divided, one way in, one way out
But which one do I enter to find my out and shout
To find my way out of here is all I want to do
If I ever come back is the bigger goal, then I'll kick the other shoe

The food they try to feed us is something other wouldn't you say
Something late yesterday will come back up to haunt me again
I hope I never see this again, oh but I probably will
They repeat and repeat that something again, and again I'll say, oh no please, no way

Here it is again, that food and still on the fence
Trying to find another way out is a must for me this day
This fence just won't part for me; I'll try going under and maybe find my way out
I'll put that food on the other side and maybe the ants will haul it away.

I came to the top to get my bearings
Adrift in a hostile sea of brick and tile
Must find my way out of this crazy place
It means to get to me good just after awhile

The clouds outside are piling up, dark clouds adrift in a crowded sky
A storm is coming, if I stay by the fence I'll probably get wet
The drops are hitting the ground a little at a time
Getting harder now, I must leave the fence, but here I sit but why

Wait a minute, its only pigeons dropping their shit on me
Got to move away from here, its getting pretty heavy now
Its in my face and now I can't see
Here they come again, I'll have to get the plow.

Keep the music flowing I don't dance there anymore
I'm old and feeble in my prime and really much too sore
One day I'll find a new rhythm, one we can all dance to
The sounds just keep on beating out, here and past the moon.

Next time I die I'll try not to come back here anymore
This place can be hazardous to your health
The heat is horrendous, the food will rot you to the core
Trying to stay cool will surely eat at your wealth

They say I'm getting rather prolific, can't stop writing anymore
The words they come, then they go, I try to jot them down as I see them
The pencil it needs sharpening, I'll wait til its just a stub
One more line should do it, then lay my pencil down on the shore.

Just can't get any sleep at night the sun keeps Betting in my way

I look up at the fish in the sea and wonder where I'm going wrong this day

I don't seem to make much sense any more but I'll try it again before I sway away

I think I've had it folks, I'll go a little deeper where the bigger fish are there to play

One more time and I have to go

I'll try to keep the music in my head

I listen intently but all I hear are the ocean waves

I'd much rather be dead instead

I have to stop this now, I'm going too deep and the lack of oxygen is getting to me

I'll turn the page and see what happens

I've been under much too long and damn I got to pee

Now they say I have narcosis, too much time in the sea

Not another breath for me, let me say that again, not another breath for me.

As I was walking up the stairs
I met a man who wasn't there
He wasn't there again today
I wish, I wish he'd go away.

Here I sit all broken hearted, this too shall pass is what they say

But the tears keep coming no end in sight

The promises are broken, it hurts deep down inside

Try to find the way to a better life, but right now I see there's just no way


The south pacific is beautiful

The islands whisper sweet nothings in my heart

They beckon my return some day, the call of Tahiti is always there

Fiji is there and Mo'orea the warm waters and diving again

Is there a way to go back, I wish, oh I wish, but do I dare?


The broken hearts would be mended, a life on the beach is there

All is forgotten in the warm sands, no memories are needed in this land

New ones will come in time, let yourself sink into the music

A special love for the islands, my mind goes back and again I care.

Two stanchions sit proudly atop the castle wall divided perfectly for watching
over the river Thames
One disappears, the other looks back and says rather humbly, "There's only me."
Looking down again and surprisingly finds there's nobody there to call, it's now
a big mall.
No place to sit anymore, it all fell down to the sea.

The river Thames has all dried up and nothing left of the castles that be
A big parking lot for the mall is all there is
And me, dried up old me; returnin8 again to watch the river, has nothing to see
I may return again after I'm dead and reunite the cancers in me.

That's all there is for now don't you see, I died, it finally got to me
I won't come back to the river no more for now, there's nothing to see
It's all been a dream, I'm still here, I didn't die this time
And the river, the Thames is still playing the music you hear in rhyme.

The stanchions are back for another tour
This poem is all I can do for now
The arthritis in my fingers gets rather sore
They get locked up, I can't move them and have to cancel the tour.

Sometimes I sleep in the morning
Sometimes I sleep in the night
Sometimes I just don't sleep at all
It's too much trouble for my mind in the light.

Bob sleeps all the time
A cadaver in the making it is
Never opens an eye to see the day
Such a life should be a crime.

I try not to let people see me sleep
It's an old weakness I seem to have
The words still come when my eyes are closed
Its then when the words come out pretty deep

Bob would make a good poet
His words are deep when they arrive
I'll go back to sleep again and try to mimic
Now I can't sleep, wouldn't you know it.

F . L .   R I K E R

The skies are emitting an eerie Blow of colors I've never seen before
I'm not looking through the eyes of me
Thru my eyes are the hues I could not know
The colors are blinding, now I can't see.

Travelers from afar are here again changing our planet as they will
I welcome these travelers they'll take me home
Home to where the colors are new to my mind all I need to do is be still
They warm my heart as it never was, no more alone, no more to kill.

There's nothing left for me here in this place
My heart has been worn to a frazzle
My mind is anxious and willing to go
Again I'll go home with what's left of me and my mind can still keep pace.

Old age is no place I want to be, all alone and in the dark
Take me home I beckon you, take me back on this day
If I must die, I'll be at ease, no more pain if that be the way
Past the stars is where I'll go then, to live forever and a day.

Back to my room where the covers are deep
To sleep again, I'll try to make it
The dreams will come and I'll wonder off
Maybe visit old friends as I see fit.

Sleeping a lot is not something I like to do
It bothers me that I'm not aware
I may sleep pretty sound and not hear a thing
Then they'll sneak up on me if they dare.

I could be dead when I wake up
Not an area of life that appeals to me
It may take one more time in somber land
But if that's the way it would happen to be, then just let it, let it be

I came down to the field to get peace and quiet
Something I need in my old age
Sitting on the catchers mound is a dangerous place to be
Exposed there all alone, there should be a cage.

I was hit twice in that open spot
Those wheelchairs run blind on the corner at night
It was a new chair for me until now
Only hit twice, that's some though not a lot.

It will happen again, oh I'm sure it will
This is not a safe place to be
I gotta go back to the fence
And if they hit me there I'll just take another pill

It's getting too crowded down here, now I gotta go

Back up to my bed where I can be alone

The pages are adding up and there will be more

The words are just shooting out, must finish this before the first snow.


I look around again and they're all gone

This park is mine and I say so

Alone again to write another poem

I'm thinking again what could go wrong.


Well it went wrong, my pencil broke

What more could there be?

I need a break, more coffee I have to make

Mr. Coffee is what they call me, I drink until dawn

Bring it again 'til it fills me, and again and again 'til I can't see.

It was so cloudy last night the sun was obscured completely

The shadows were gone and no light from the sky what so ever

We're all in the dark on this night, it could be this will last forever

Forever and a day some say, its midnight

Again and again, the days have disappeared

And now not a one can see.

The sun came out at midnight to the open astonishment of all
Eyelids popped open everywhere, no one was ready for this bright light from the sky
The flames from the sun were hurting my eyes, and again the eyelids were closing
The countless days of sun were depressing and again no one could see and now
the struggle to understand why.

This universe is going backwards, my mind is spinning out of control
I keep digging deeper and deeper, I'll never get out of this hole
The words keep pressing through, and it's a hassle to make them rhyme
I'll make it end here and now for my brain is about out of time.

In the closed dark spaces of my mind
I feel the deepening horror
Digging blood dripping pitchforks
Torture me throughout my whole
Empty blackened walls they now surround me
Reaching hopelessly for a blood soaked door.

In this dreadful while of time
I'll now spend with the devil in my soul
Never ending hell is all that's left for me
Nothing left of the world I know, from now I'll never see.

The gates are still locked, they still won't let me out
Oregon seems so very far away
I'll never get there at the rate I'm Boing
Somethings gotta happen I mean to say.

Travel plans are in the making
Suitcases packed and ready
Somehow I'll get through these bars
Another beer and just hold steady.

On the left side of my brain there is nothing right

On the right side there is nothing left

These poems all come from the right side so I can't really be held accountable

The poems will go on 'til all are left or again 'til there is nothing right, and I'll go on


I blew my nose and a tooth came out, that's ok

My teeth are all on the right, they'll all fall out 'til there is nothing left


And now let's go back to my brain

Just turn the page and everything is on the right again and we'll go on

My nose, there's not much left of that either

It's all connected, mostly on the right

Want more?

My words are silent for the days going forward
Only the sounds of a man with no home
Alone into the darkness and so I sail
No words could there be, adrift, again and again, pounding that rusty nail.

The sails are down, the wind picking up
Forever adrift on the rough sea waves
It may last forever in my turbulent mind
No safe haven anywhere, my minds gone to waste
No more home for this one of a kind.

I put a band aid on my hemorrhoids tonight and lo and behold another tooth fell out
They all came out in no time, more band aids I require before I short
Maybe I'll need a sling before it's all over
A sling for my hemorrhoids in a pouch.

I'll hang them on my front door and just over night
The tooth fairy should proclaim, "What do I do now?"
More band aids she'll leave, and a quarter for each and under my pillow they went
My hemorrhoids still hurt, more band aids are needed, but my tooth fairy is
uglier than a cow.

Oops, I had a bad dream last night, I dreamed I fell out of bed
Took most of the side table with me, all my Dr. Pepper and everything went
Oops, it wasn't a dream and there I lay, soaking wet and no longer in bed
All the nursing cohorts came to see, they helped me up and comforted me.

I'll go down for a cigarette to calm me down
Oops, I'm out of cigarettes, picking butts right off the ground
Oh what a day this is gonna be.

One day all this bullshit and my cancer will get me

I wait patiently for its call, I can hear the sound of death close by

As I meet it head on and have to wait no more

I'll go to the top and greet my fate, looking forward to the long drop to the sea

All the turmoil in my brain will have to cease

There's not much left of the one called me.

I have a debilitating re-occurrence of what they call restless leg

It's a weird thing where your leg just wants to keep moving

My wife told me a sure fire cure that works every time

A good shit is what she said so I went and forced it out 'til I had to beg.

The next day, I sat there and my leg started to move

No no no not again is all I said

I stayed put and just let it happen and there goes my leg without me.

More band aids for my hemorrhoids and now down to one leg

I had about enough of this so now there is no longer a we

My leg just keeps moving, down the hall it went

All those band aids well, just money well spent.

Weight of time itself is a powerful tool
It takes all the knowledge you've earned and saved over the years
Compressing it down to a single drop 'til no one can see what you know, not even your peers

The weight of time is pressing me down, much further than I want to be
I have to stop time and slow down this freefall, get back up where I can see.

The sun set on my mind years ago
Nothin8 but ideas and stars are left for me
No place to go and a lot of time to get there
Maybe I can brake these chains of time and be free of this place forever
Walk right out the door and come back here again never
I'm willing to go and ready to travel but this time to where.

I have a mixed up mind that's for sure
Ideas just pop right in but now there's no way out
Trapped in a storm of heavy clouds and find there's just no cure
Someday more clouds will form and raindrops will fall at their leisure
I'll venture out and absorb all I can, deep to the bone is my pleasure.

Now here I am one leg, a dozen band aids on my hemorrhoids and now I can't shit
I better go see a doctor soon before I can't take it anymore
That doctor ripped all the band aids off and said, "Ok, we'll try a tourniquet."
So he tied the knot and said go home, everything will fall off soon and you'll just be a little sore.

So I went home and true to the doctor's word, everything fell off and damn I'm sore, can't shit
So now I can't stand, can't sit, can't shit, and I can no longer reach the door
My hemorrhoids came off and now there's piles 3 feet thick wall to wall all the way to the door
So that's the end of my hemorrhoids folks and there's my restless leg- back knocking at the door for more.

Raindrops keep falling everywhere, even outside the cage we're in

Raindrops are free, they're welcome in here even past the guards wherever they be

It used to rain in space so very long ago, all the planets had raindrops before they hit the sun

The rains were there way past Pluto and into the emptiness we see

Our universe is just a tiny drop in the circle of existence

A drop destined to repeat itself time after time, it's the never ending beauty of the dance

A dance I've seen before in my travels through space

For I've been there many times, going slower and slower for this is not a race

The guards will disappear and the rain will still fall

Leaving puddles on the landscape of any planet we're on

The guards have nothing to protect, the fences are down, and the sands of the hourglass have taken all

Time itself will disappear, leaving just our dots to forever move on.

Writing is easy, just close your mouth and open your mind
The words will come and you may be surprised.

We need new chairs down here, we only have two

Sink your ass in one and it'll put you right on the ground

They're old and worn out and not very sturdy at all

Not a place to relax at all, new chairs are needed here, enough to go around.

I have to put my pencil down and get more coffee in me
They call me Mr. Coffee, now I have to live up to that name
I'll empty the pot in no time to the astonishment of all
Mr. Coffee is at it again and that name suits me to a tee
I have to get more coffee in me and get ready for tomorrow
Tomorrow is a whole new game.

I came to the fence to think and watch the stars' play
I find the big dipper, little dipper, and other forms there are
Can't see the stars yet, it's way too early
So it's just me and my thoughts to wait for another day.

No love to hold me, no paycheck to wait for
Just me and my mind to welcome the stars
A long wait, no, not at all; no crowds, no people to mix up my thoughts
My mind takes over and I have to travel, to the moon and then past mars.

Saturn is coming up fast, I'll probably get lost in the rings
I'll just keep going, holding to none
My mind is a perfect companion in my effort to get home
Past the stars and then again, through the empty void, then I know I'm close

Just me and that thin8 called time, then I know I've won
Only me and my thoughts, no one to care for
No human form can be found in this world
Then time becomes absent, a world of thought, not even a sun.

F.L. RIKER

I used to go up to the fence at night
My only chance to be alone
Others found out where I was
Now I no longer have a home.

One, two, three, more, they started to accumulate
Being alone at the fence is now something new
Still go up once in awhile just to look through the bars
Enter my dreams and in my mind I then flew.

The big escape was on my mind, over the fence was I
Nothing holding me back this time, just gotta go, just gotta go
And away I went, past the moon and into the stars
I look back and damn I made it, out of relief a big sigh.

I come down to have a cigarette and end up helping the aides do their job

They're so ill trained for what they're supposed to do

They bring the vets down to smoke and not at all prepared

An old vet, had no way to reach the ash tray then turned to me with one, awkward SOB.

I was down here at 2 am one night, a vet was down here smoking

It was cold that night, that vet could not get to an ash tray, no blanket and shivering like the morning dew

Common sense is all that is needed or an IQ a little higher than what we see

After awhile it really gets under my skin, maybe I've been here too long but now it's starting to upset me.

It hurts sometimes, almost enough to bring a tear to a glass eye

I can do nothing but sit here and sigh

On the application when they first apply- are you stupid? (duh duh)

Can you speak English? (si, si), you're hired

When I speak out and try to complain - you're fired

All that's really needed when they bring the vets down is cigarettes, a lighter, a blanket, and common sense

Most of the aides I've seen here lack basic understanding and are ultimately really dense.

Relax, take a minute to read a poem, it'll do your mind wonders
Nothing is more important than being steady in your job
Vacate your mind and send it to your heart
That's where the ultimate decisions are made, as easy as turning a knob.

Now your mind is empty, you can start the day anew
Nothing will make more sense to you than doing what you do
Turn the key gently and all new thoughts will then appear
Turn the key again and your heart will come shining through.

I'm back at the fence again trying to avoid the racers
They're coming at me left and right, I try to pay them no heed
I'll have to move to a safer spot soon, my nerves can't take too much of this
All this noise I try to put up with but it's definitely not in my deed.

The stars are falling from the sky, one at a time they go
Soon the sky will be empty with nothing more to show
The moon still glows but just maybe this too will not be for very long
I'll go back to my room for a bit and maybe I'll write a song.

The sparrows come in to take a bath, the bird bath is always easy

I also count the pigeons, in this place there's not much else to do

We have a bucket of water on the ground and then there's always the cool morning dew

Very polite these pigeons, they're taking turns to drink

Never shit in the drinking water or bird bath, not a drop they make

There's about 50 pigeons that live here, never leaving the home

They must be veterans, they are, friendly to a one

They get rather rambunctious at feeding time but hey, they're under their dome.

I look at the bars that hold me, and the guards with their guns go walking by
The pigeons are asleep in their quarters and now a grasshopper comes to the gate
Can't let him in, he'll never get out, this is life for most
Such is the life in this veterans' home, all we can do is wait.

My mood, not the greatest right now
The radiation side effects are taking their toll
Diarrhea 3 days now, no relief in site
It's getting to me I guess but it can't last forever
I've been down before and got up again to give it a good fight

I can take the pain, that's nothing new
I've had pain all my life and endured
The years are piling up, the stars are getting dimmer
No more travel for me, no more into the blue.

One more cigarette and back under the covers I go

There's a chill in the air, the chill of the first snow

A good hot coffee is called for, then another cup, and maybe more

I went to the window, looked up and saw the fish sliding on the ice

One of the pigeons didn't make it home last night

I think I'm getting a little frost between my ears

I'm thinking too fast, the snow is hitting with a powerful smite

One more coffee.

Clouds are piling up, rains are pouring down
Snows are drifting 6 feet deep all around
Heaven and hell are colliding, they'll meet with an astounding clash
Human life will end with a never ending smash

Life on earth is over, I guess I'll just go back to the home
The snows aren't too deep out there and I'll be under the VA dome
Lunch will be here by dinner and the pigeons love peanut butter
All this and more under the VA dome.